Get I

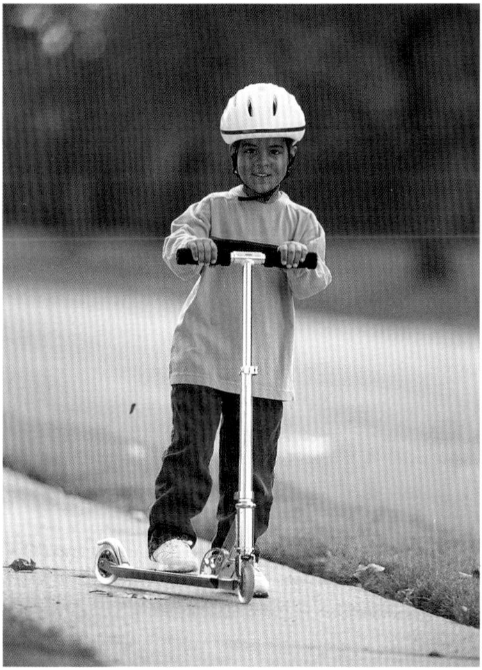

written by Pam Holden

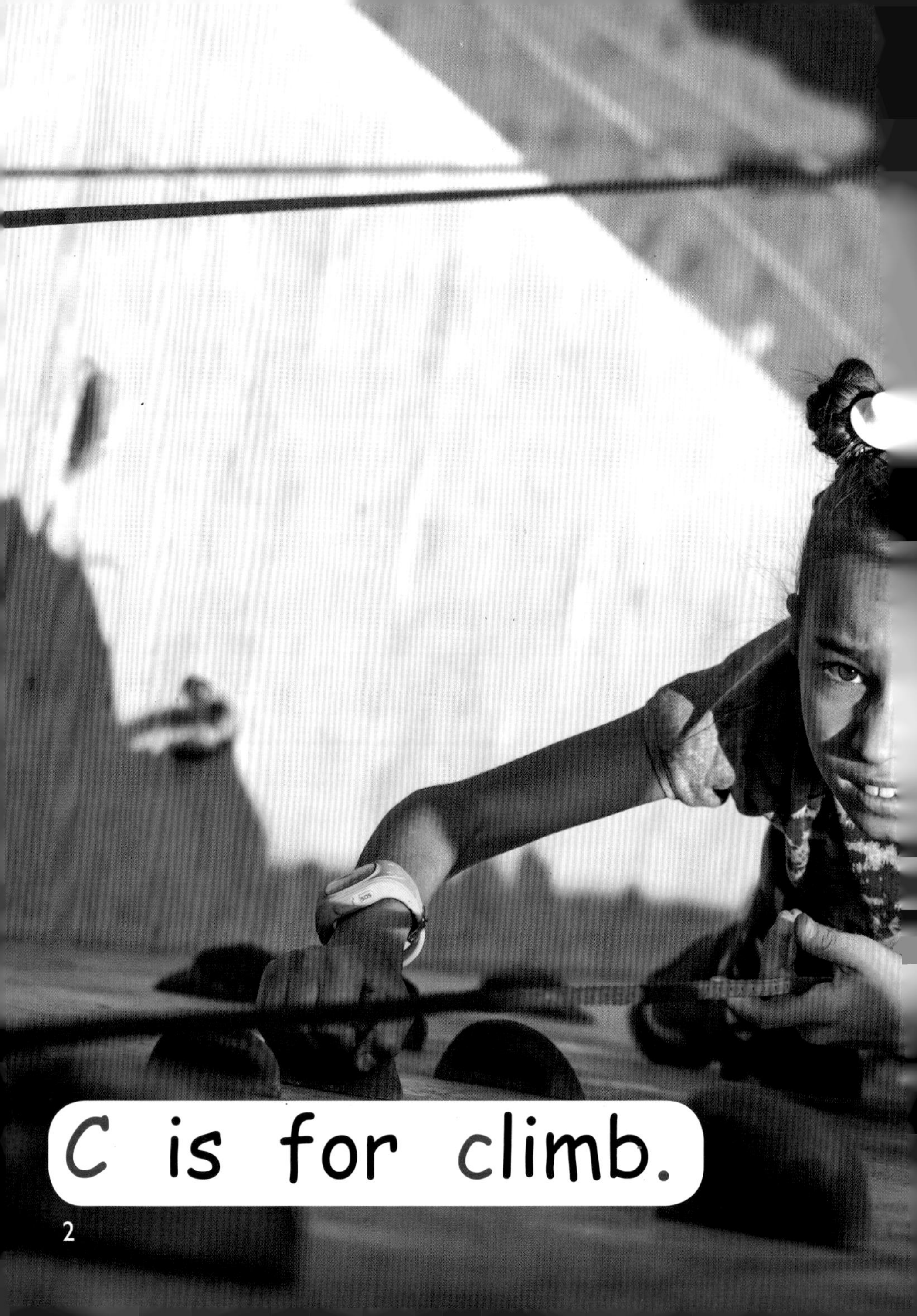

C is for climb.

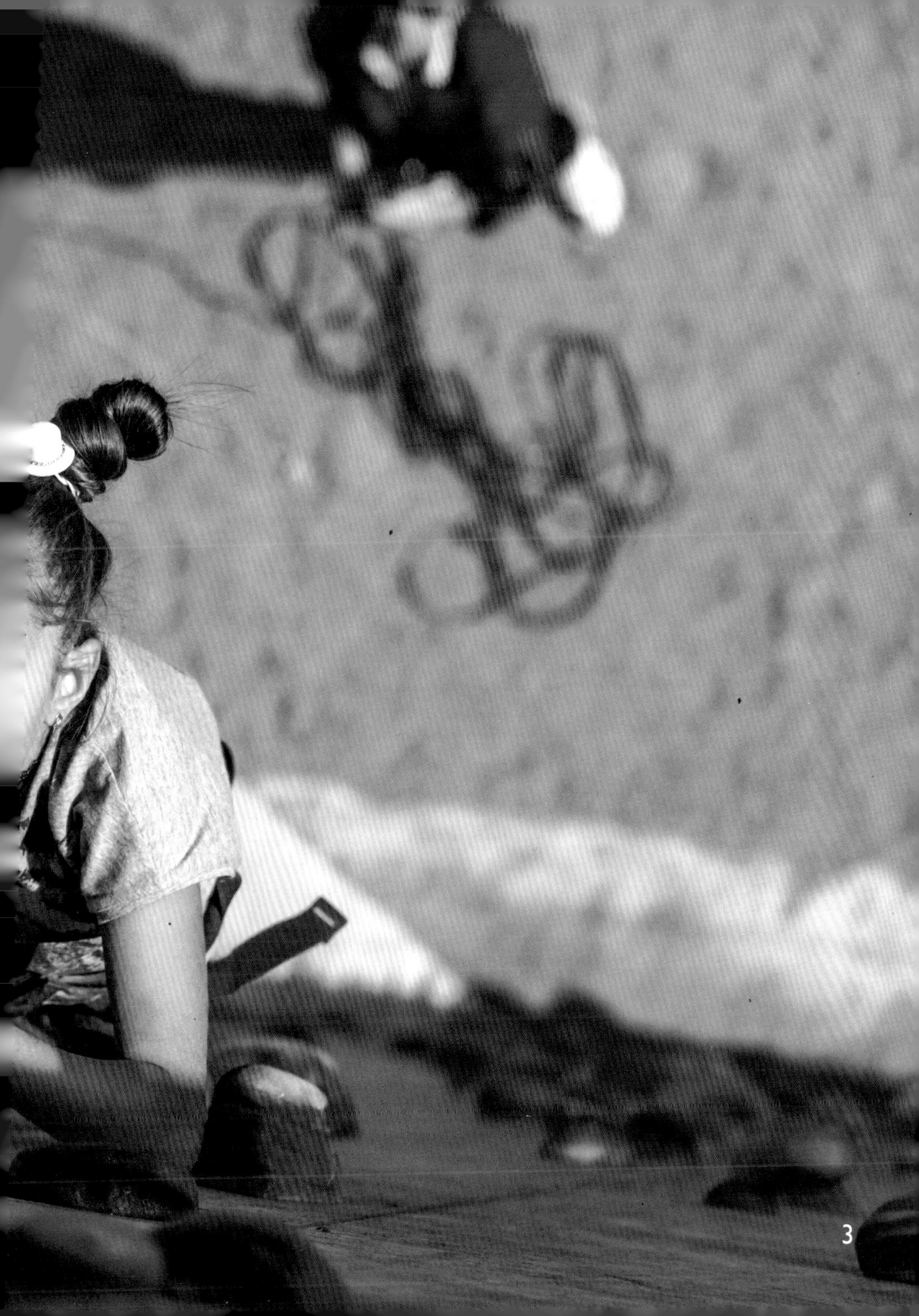

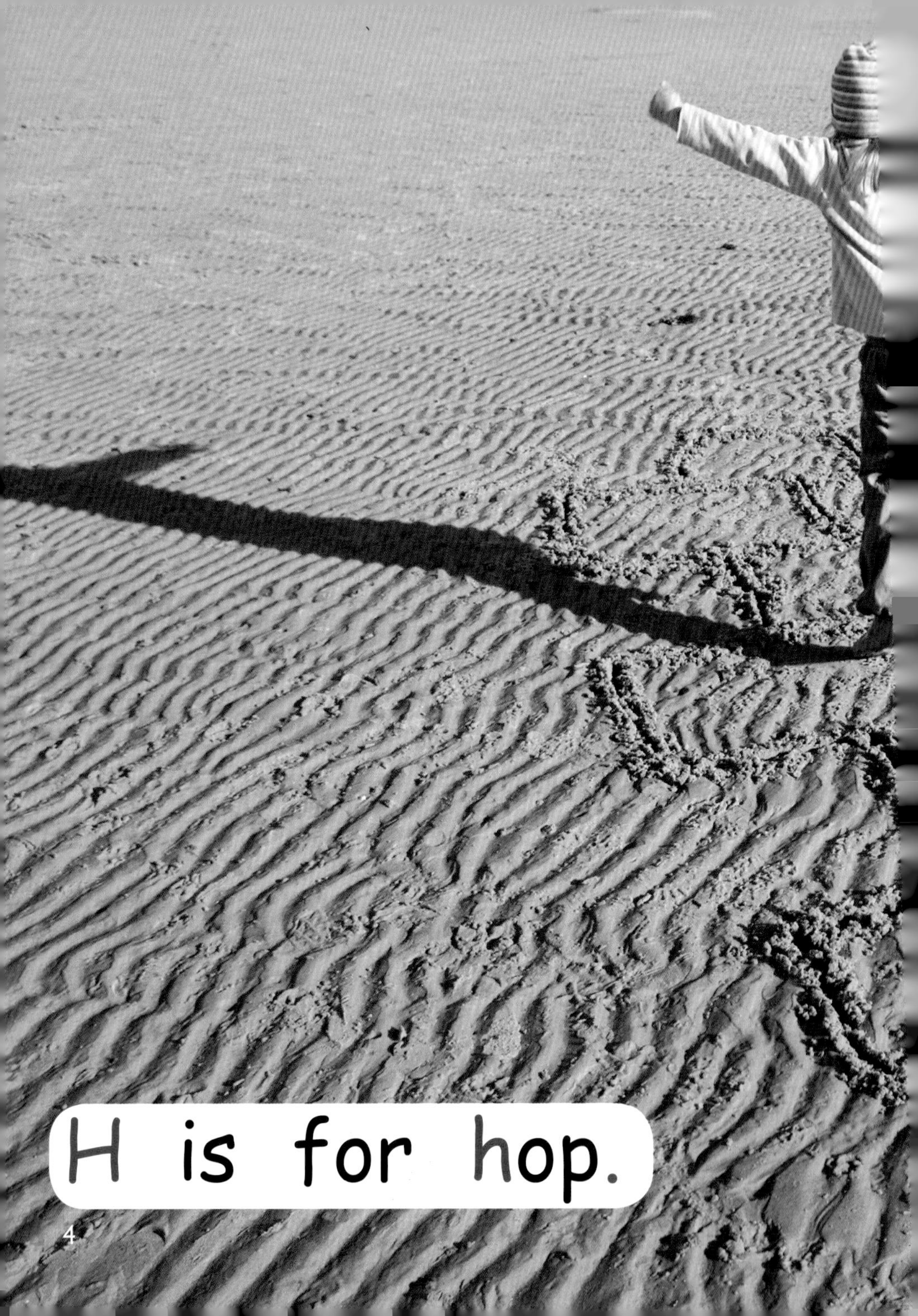

H is for hop.

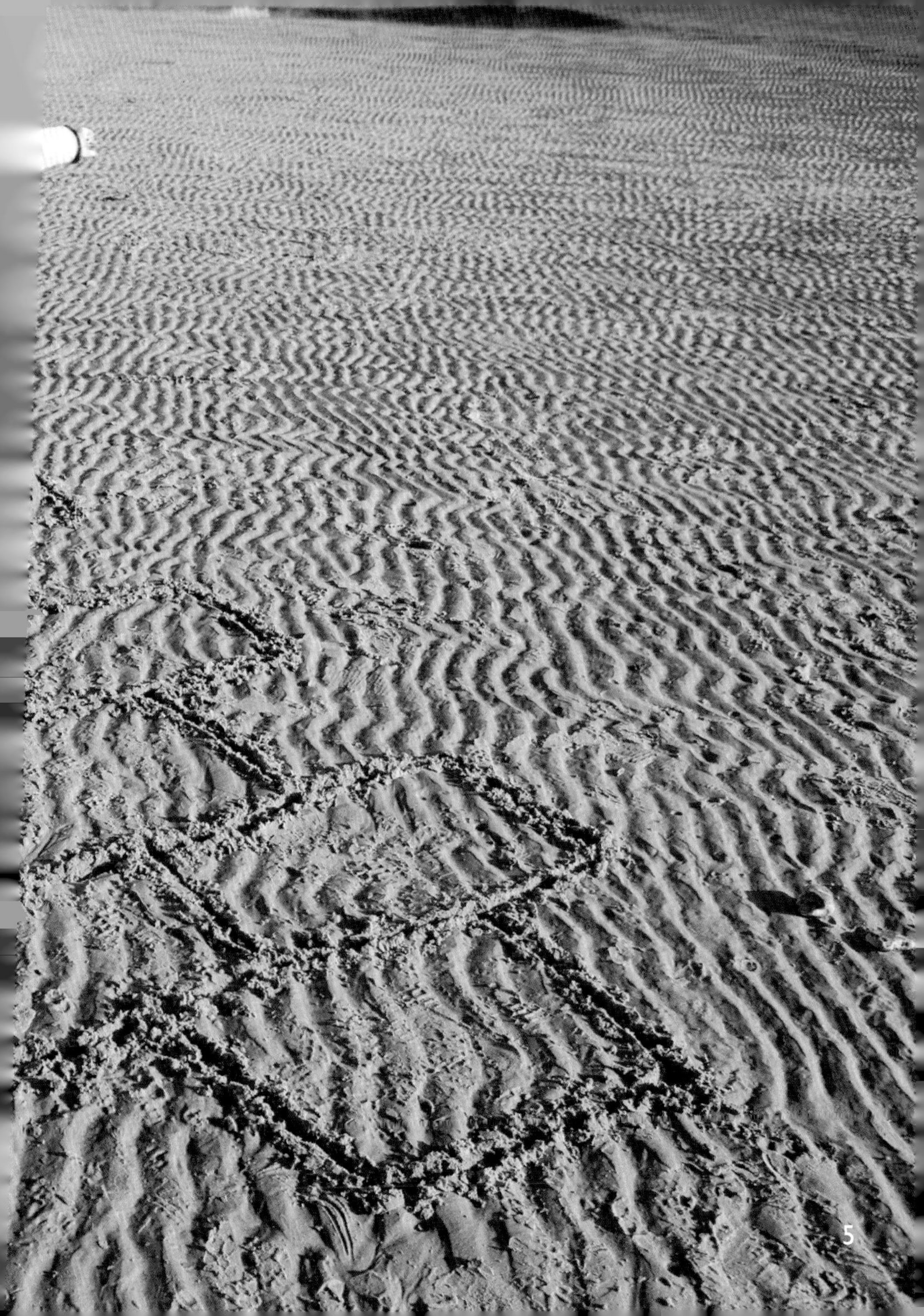

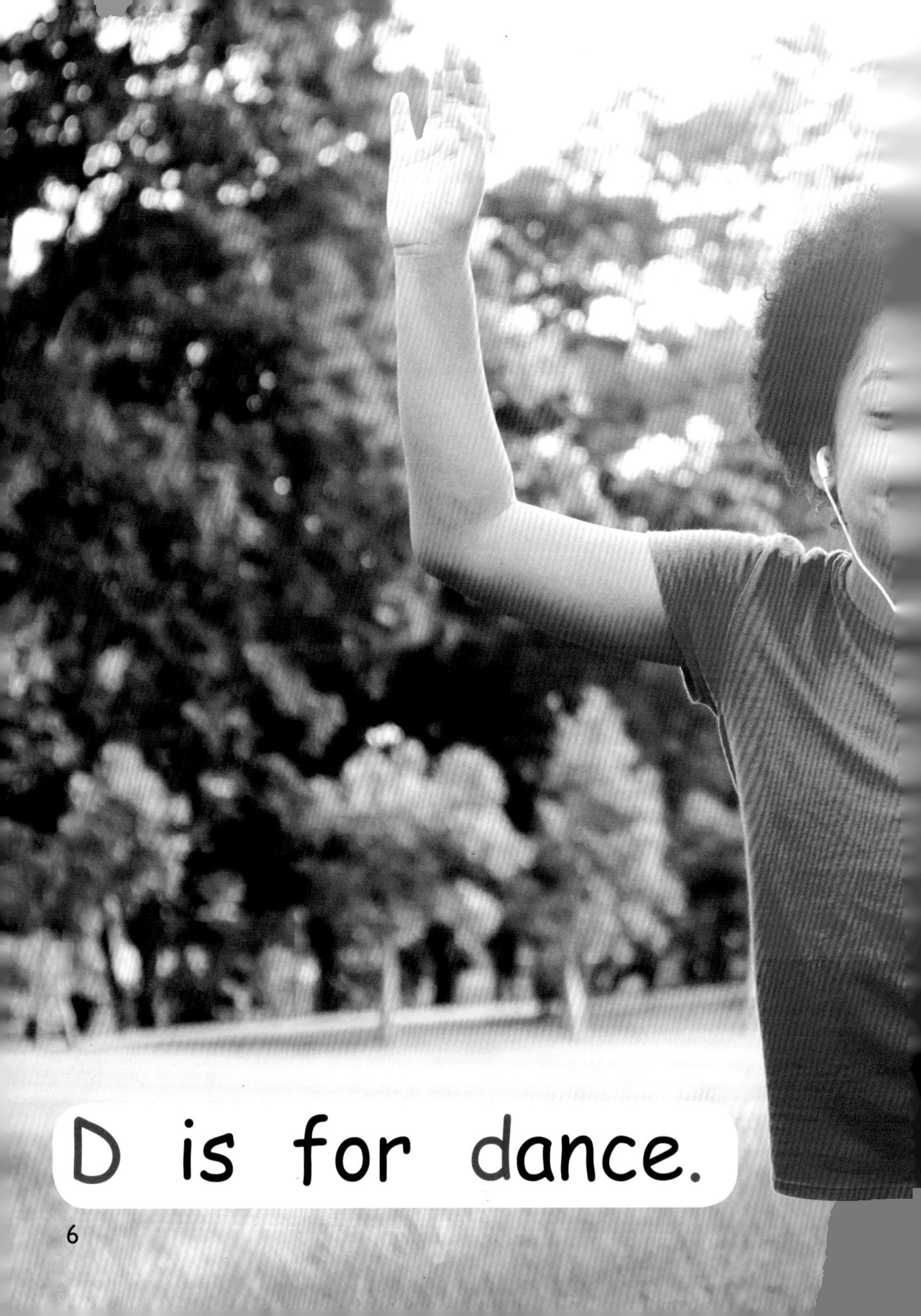

D is for dance.

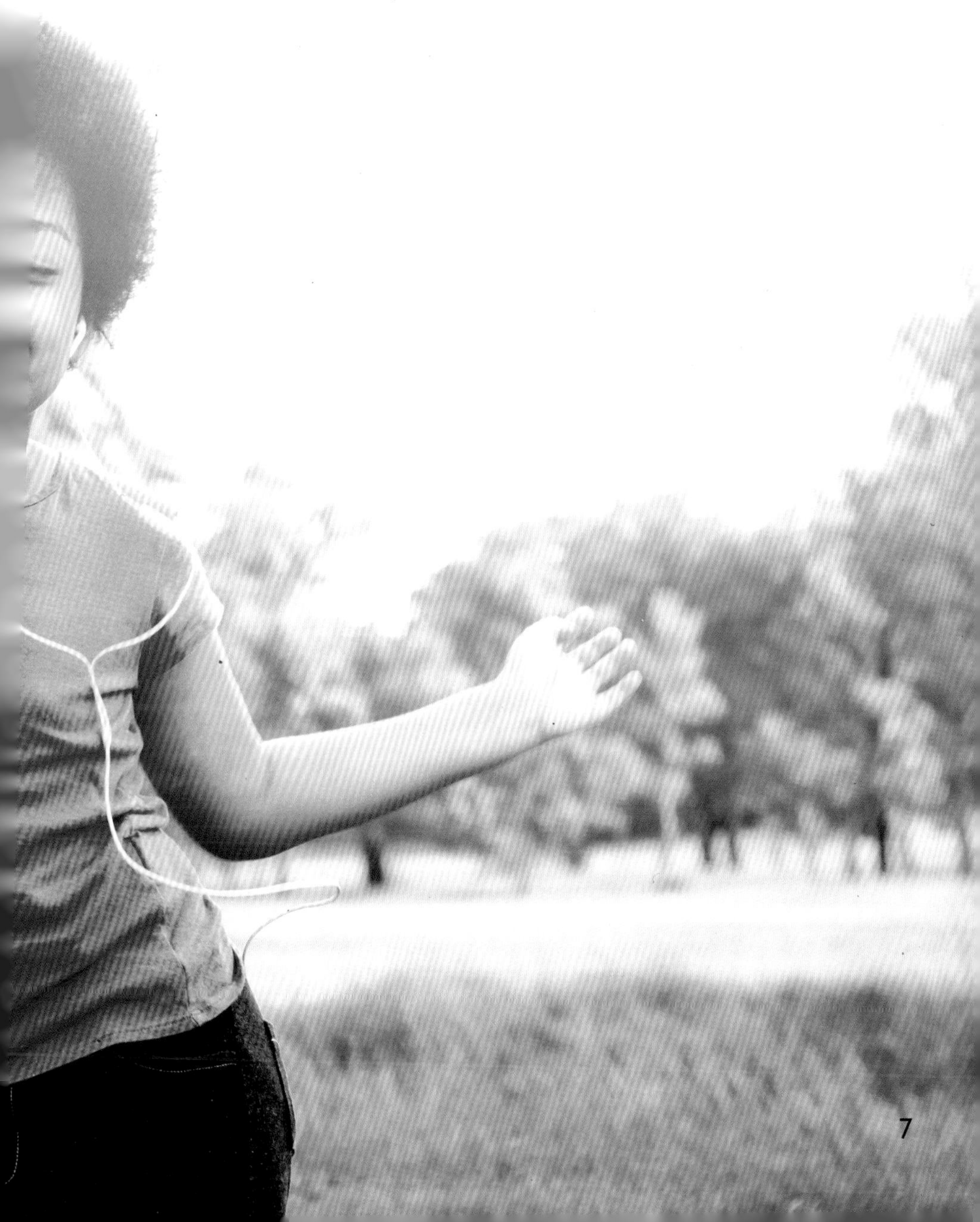

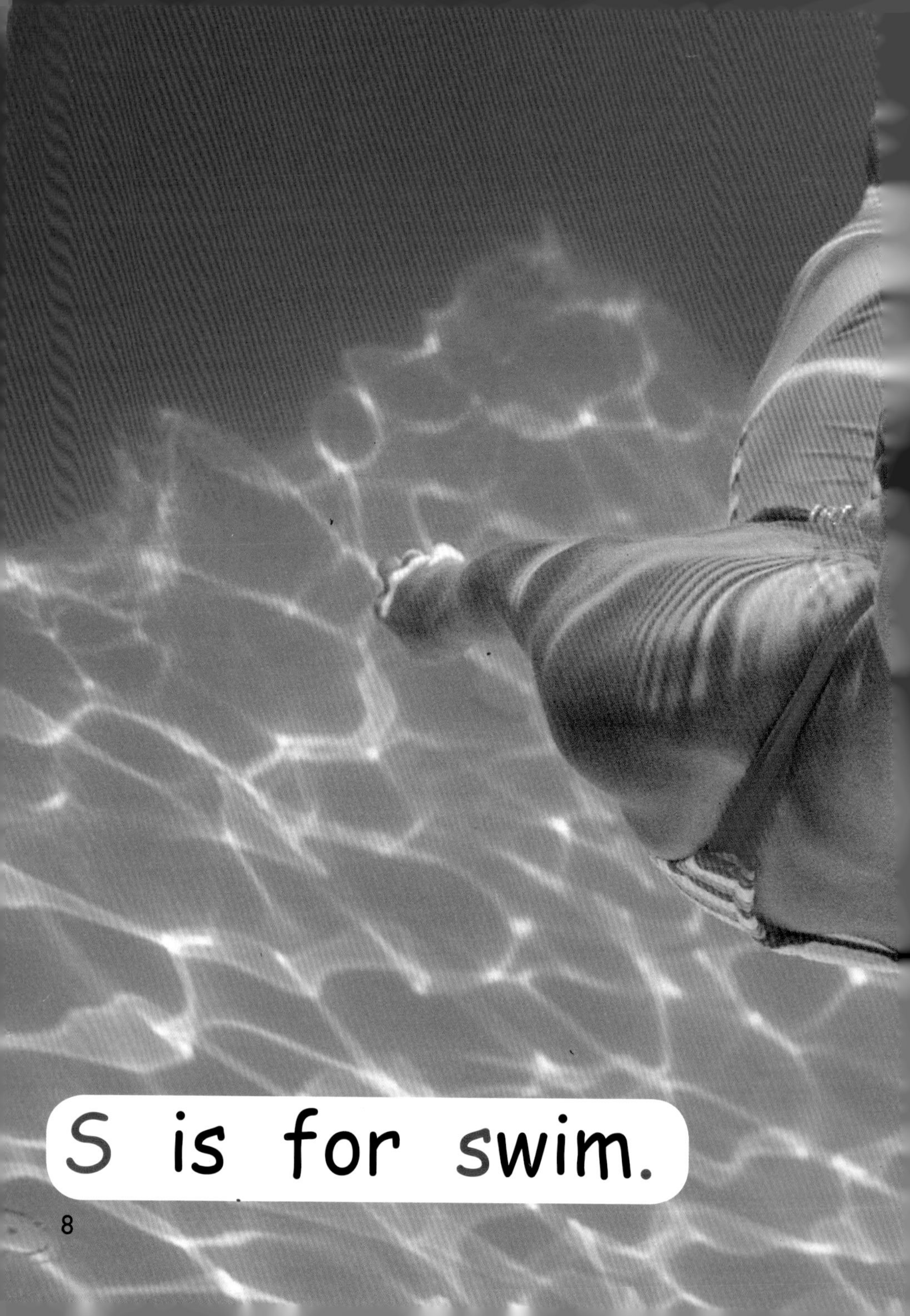

S is for swim.

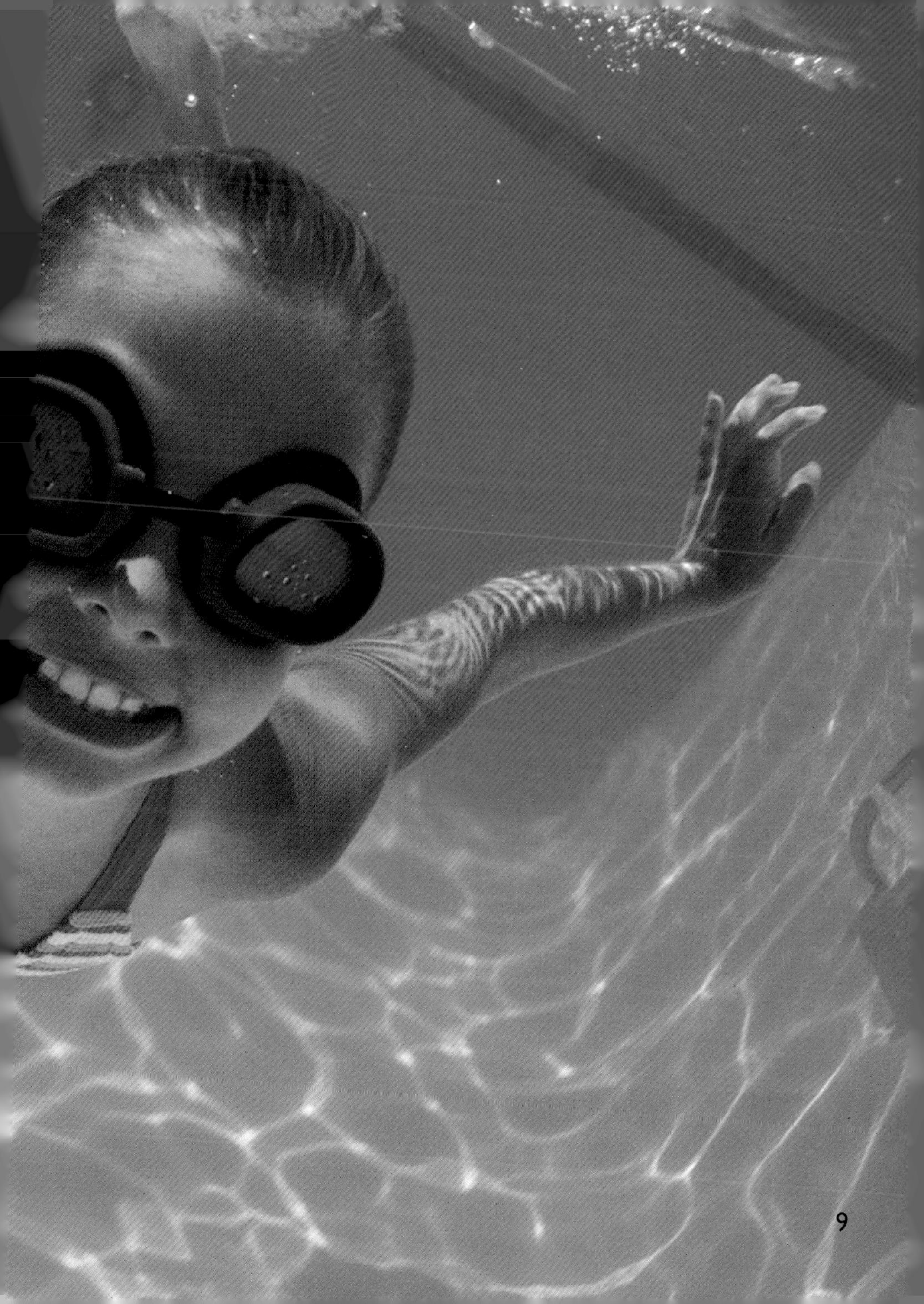

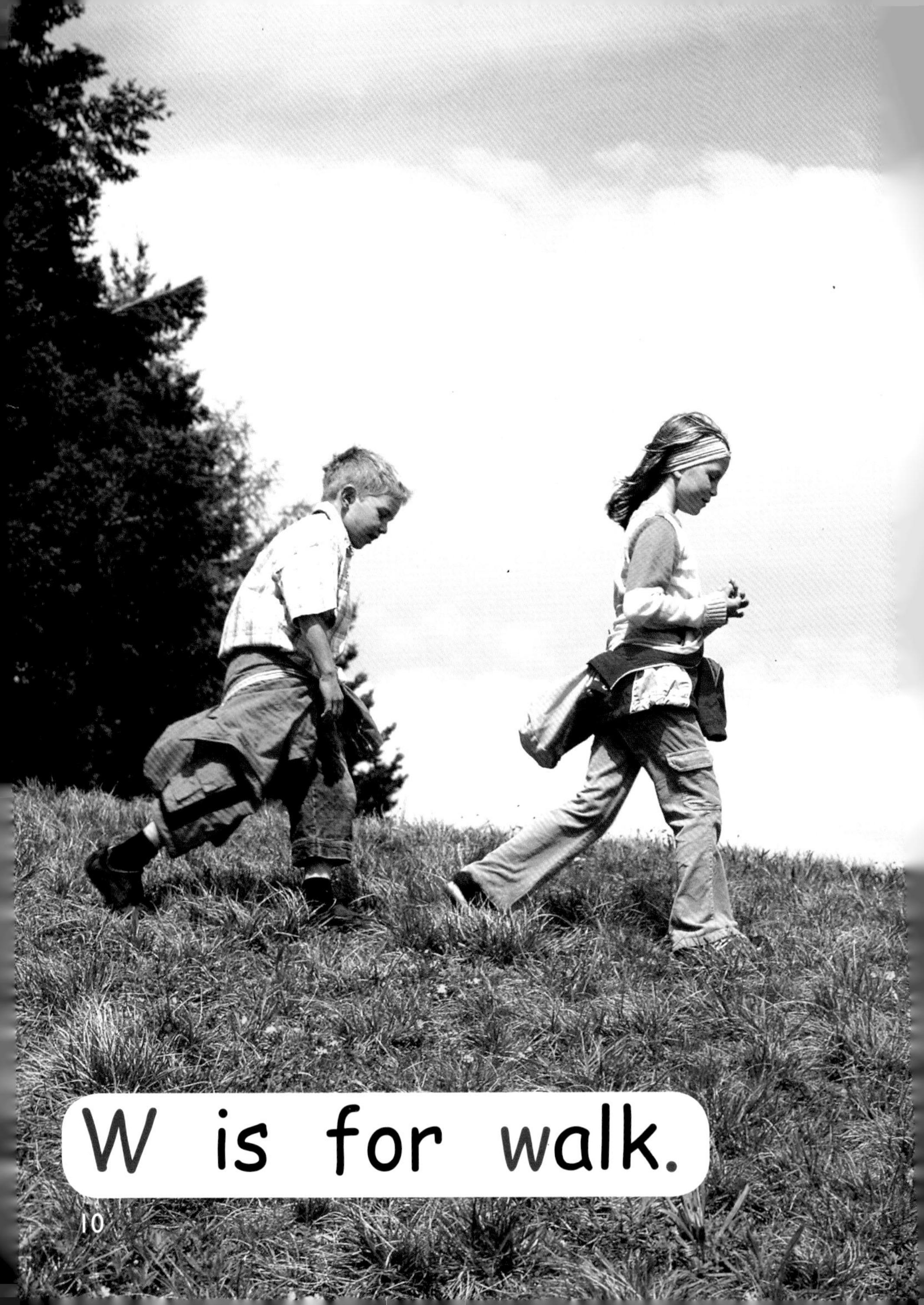

W is for walk.

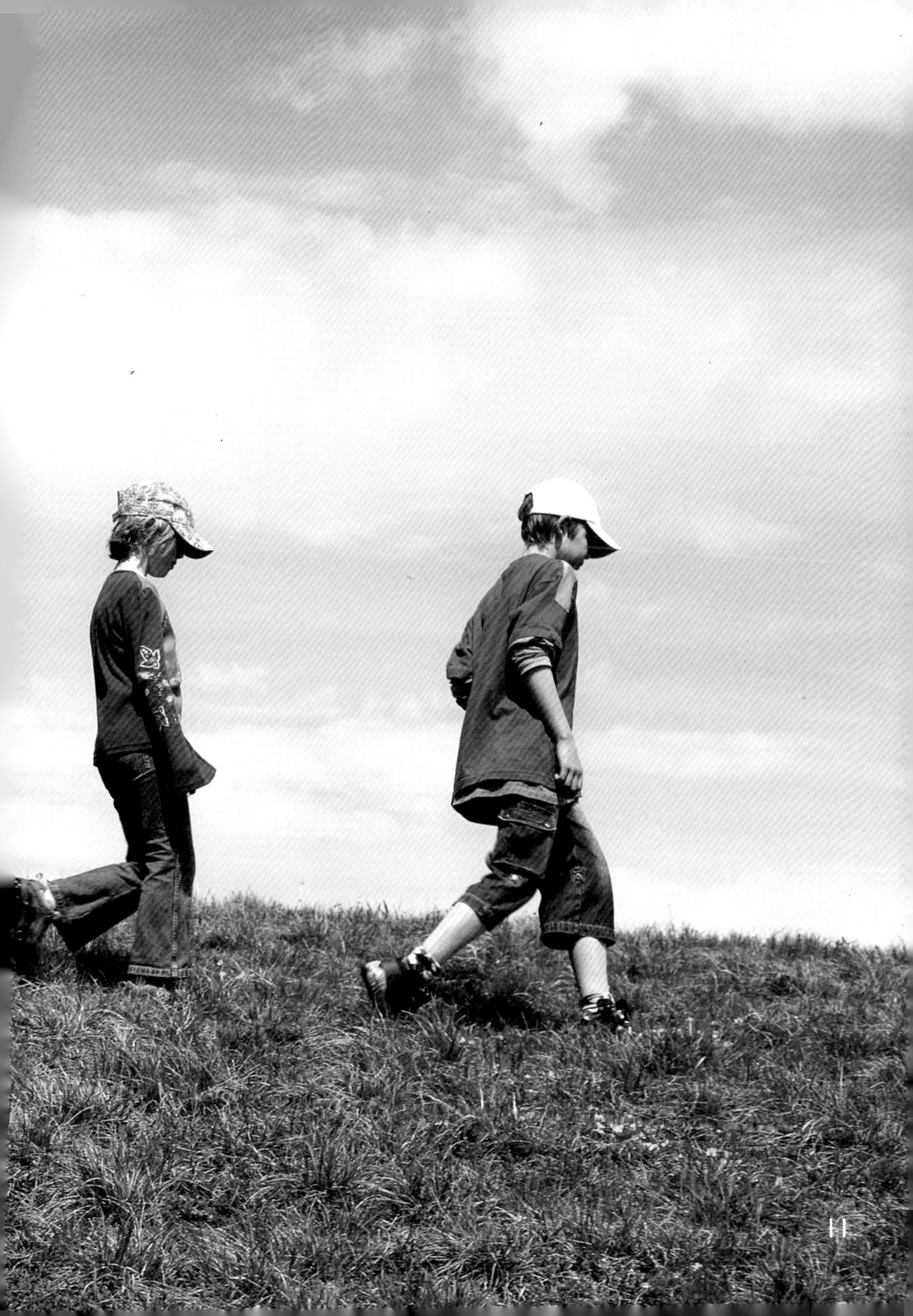

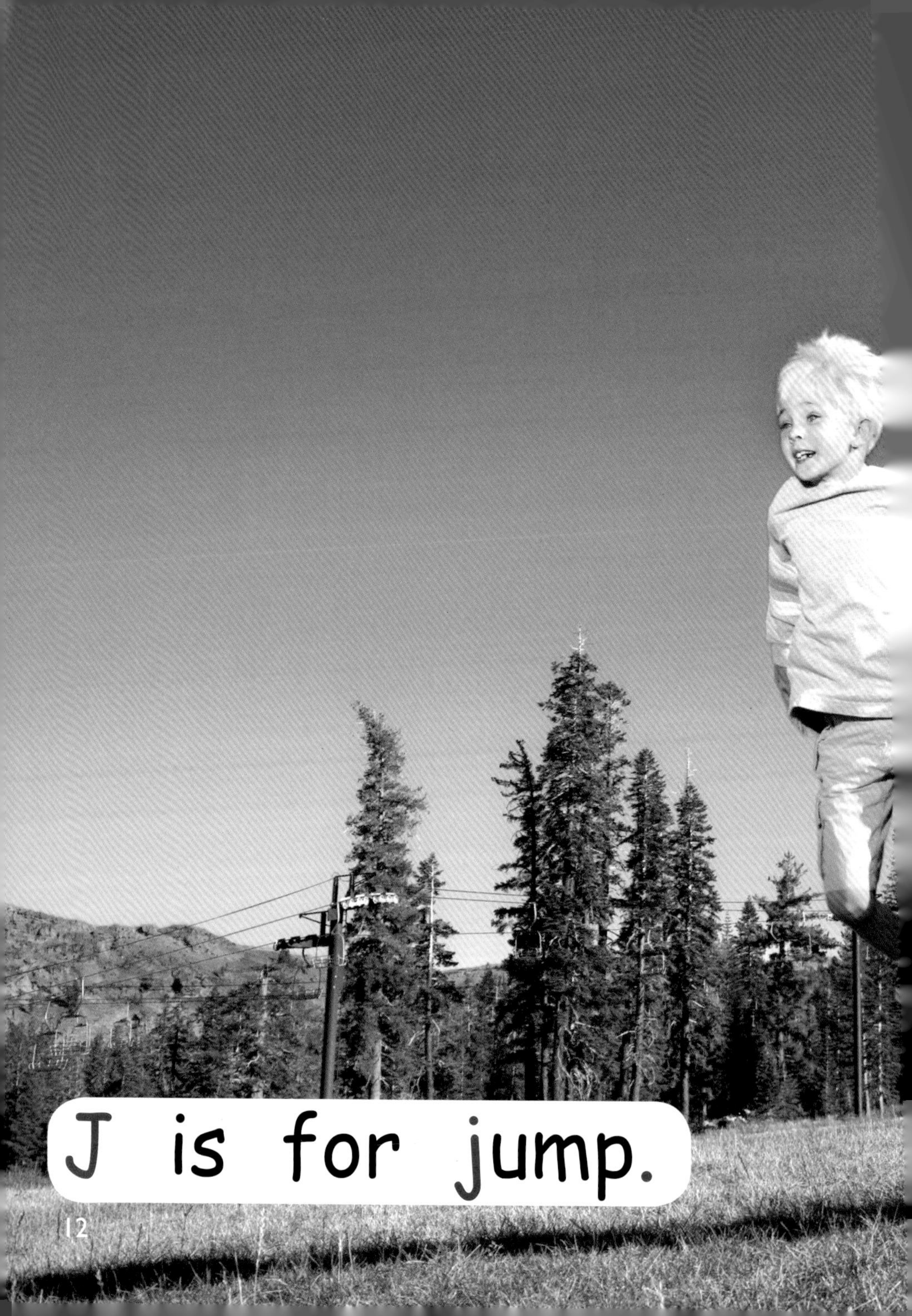

J is for jump.

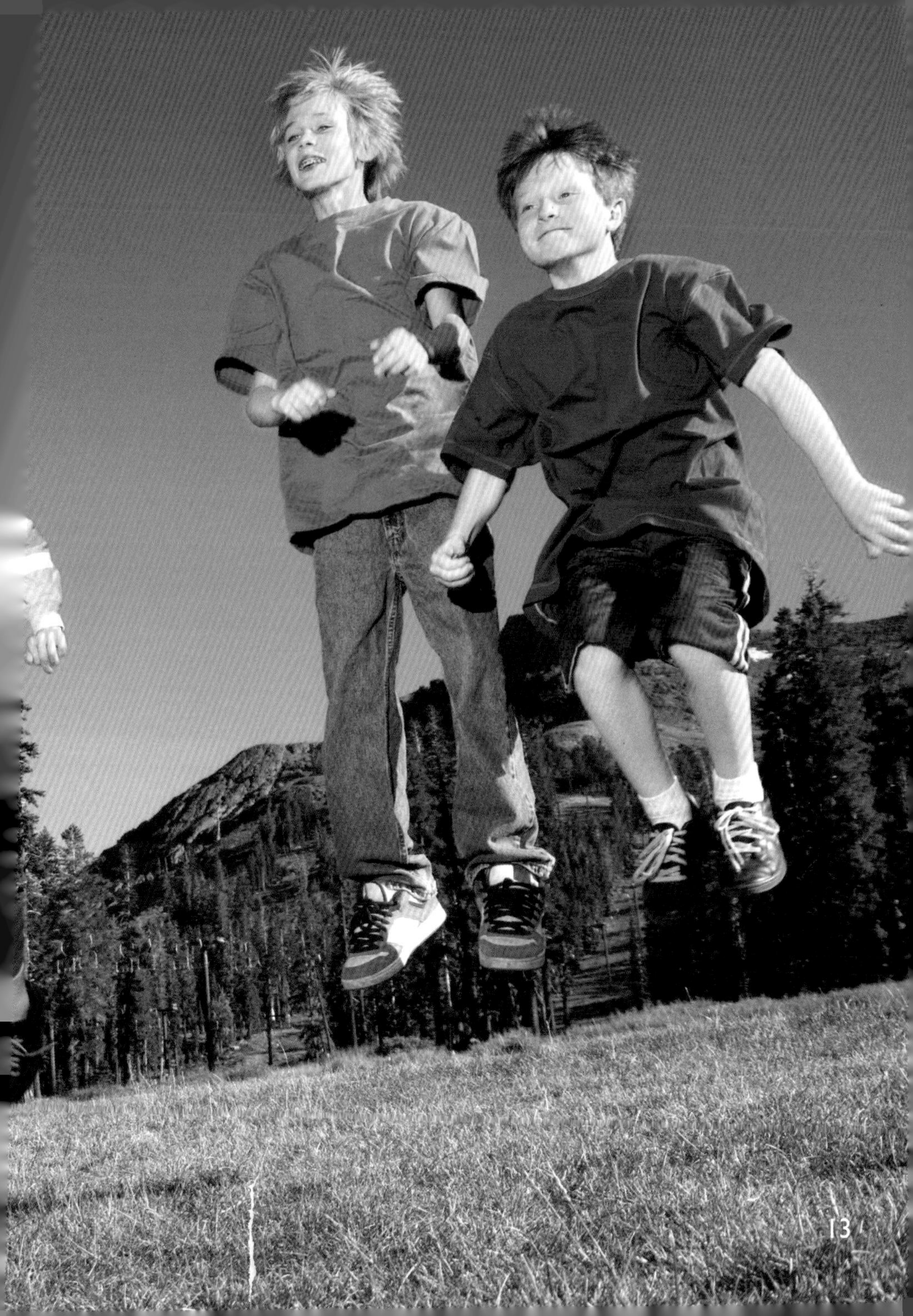

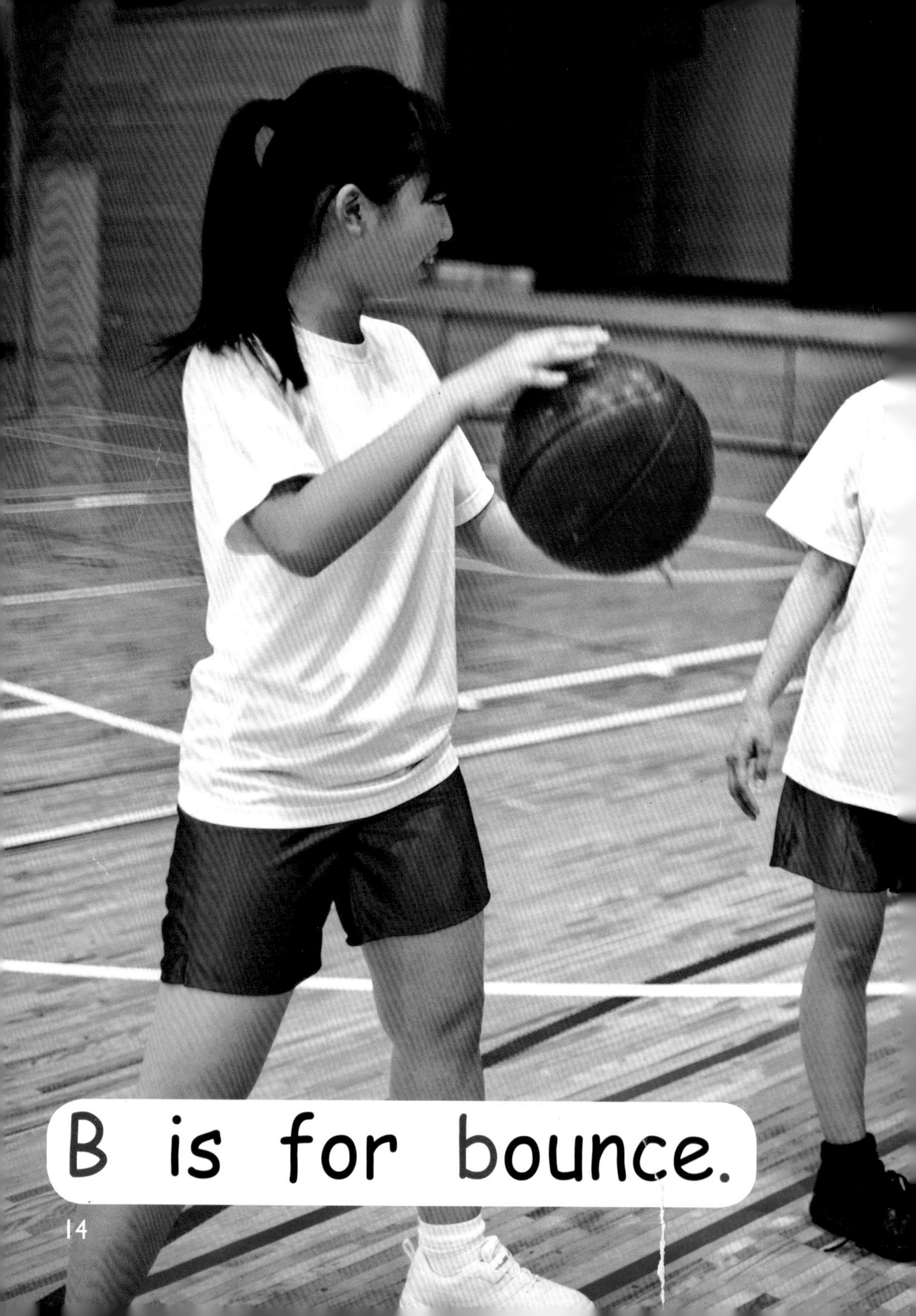

B is for bounce.

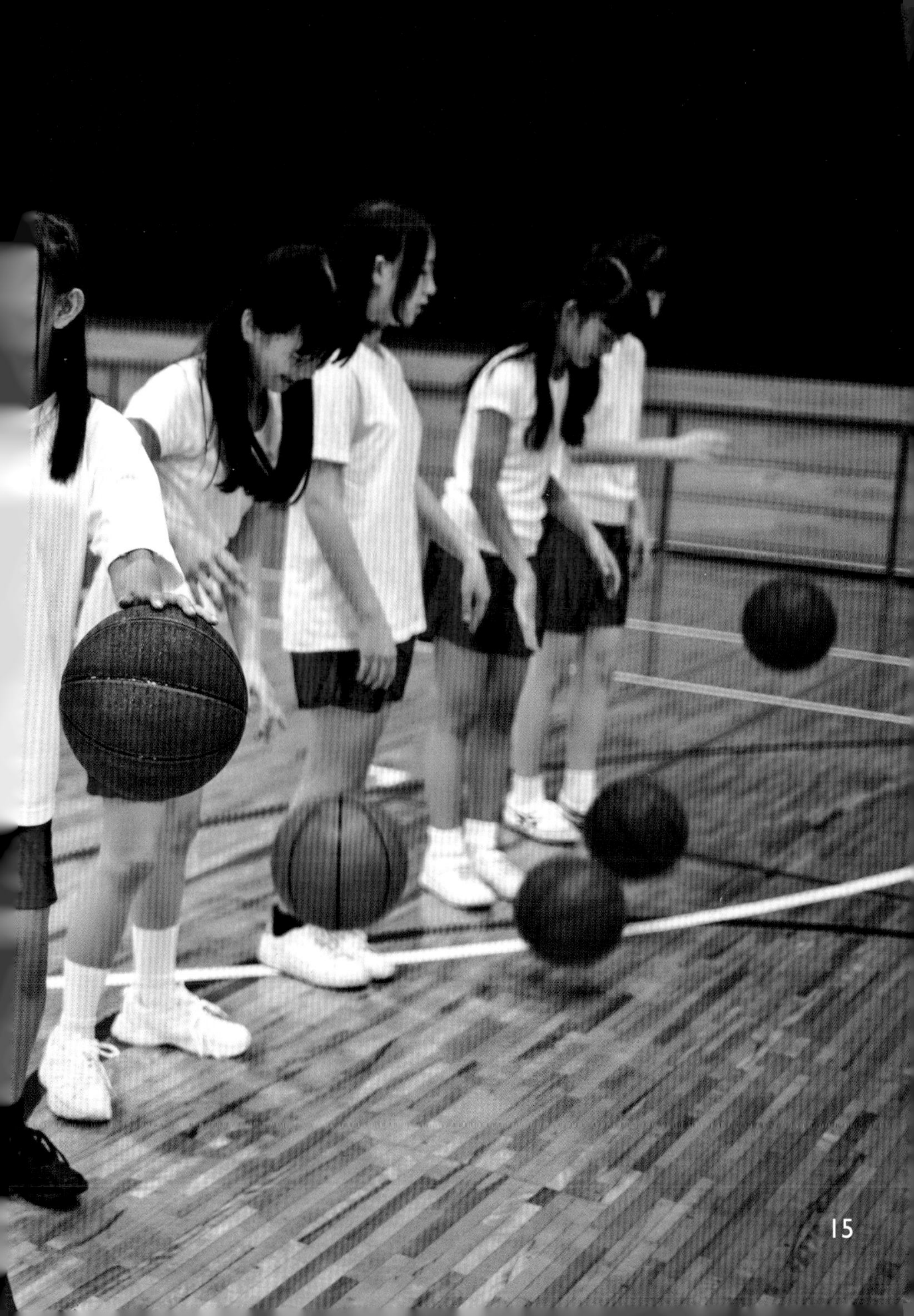

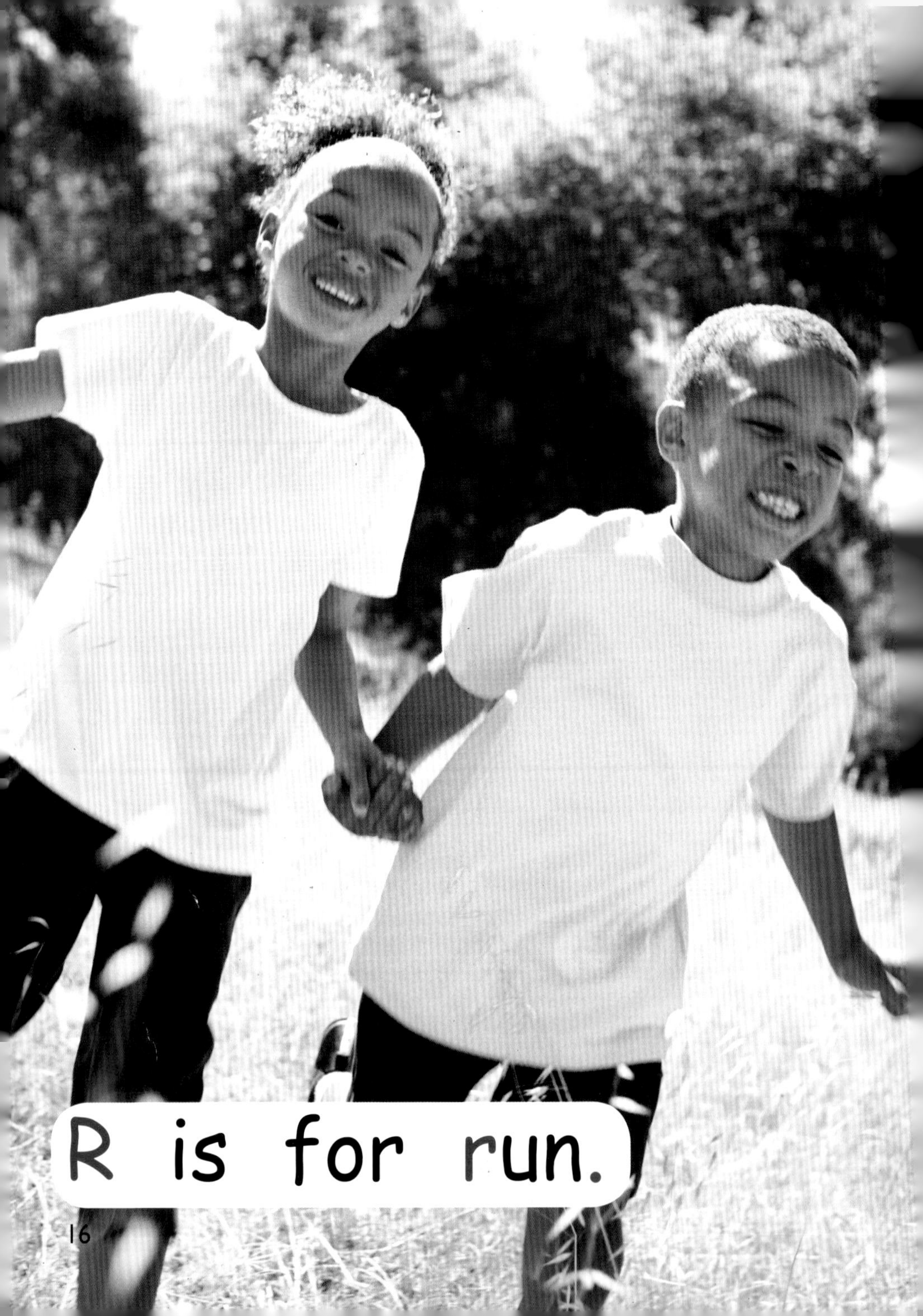

R is for run.